# What Does God Know?

# What Does God Know?

## Reconciling Divine Foreknowledge *and* Human Freedom

WILLIAM L. CRAIG

WIPF *&* STOCK · Eugene, Oregon

# INTRODUCTION

In a self-proclaimed postmodern age in which the "re-imagining" of God by anti-realists, feminists, and radical pluralists often takes bizarre and unconventional forms, the denial on the part of otherwise very conservative theologians that God is all-knowing or omniscent might seem a harmless and even welcome modification of the traditional concept of God. But it is the very seeming innocence of this alteration that should make us all the more careful. For while radical aberrations are easy to recognize and avoid, it is the subtle deviations from the truth which are more likely to lead astray and may end in ruinous pitfalls. Revisionist understandings of the traditional doctrine of divine omniscience therefore deserve to be examined with utmost scrutiny.

The contemporary critique of divine omniscience focuses on God's foreknowledge of future contingent's. By "future contingents," one means *future events that are not causally determined by present events* (for example, future free human decisions). Revisionist theologians allege that God does not know which future contingent events will happen. For example, He does not know if Hillary Clinton will decide to run for President in 2008. They also claim that God does not have hypothetical knowledge concerning which events *would* happen if certain other events were to take place. Such events are sometimes referred to as "conditional future contingents." At best He knows only what *could* happen under any set of circumstances that might exist. So, for example, He does not know what would happen if Hillary Clinton were to decide to run for President in 2008. All He knows is that she could win or lose or drop out or whatever.

Such limited knowledge on God's part has a direct impact upon the doctrines of divine sovereignty and providence. Since God lacks the hypothetical knowledge of how things would go if He were to act in certain ways, as well as foreknowledge of how things will in fact go, God can neither predict nor plan the course of future events.  As a result, God is ignorant of virtually all of humanity's future, since even a single free choice could turn history in a different direction than its present course.  Subsequent events would, as time goes on, depart increasingly from history's present trajectory.  At best God can be said to make intelligent guesses about what will happen in the near future and then react to events as they happen.  He is therefore said to be a "risk-taking" God.  Proponents of this view refer to it as "the Openness of God."  Some of the advocates of the open view of God even assert that God is sometimes wrong in His expectations of the future and therefore makes mistakes, which He later regrets.  They further allege that such a conception of God is faithful to biblical teaching.

In this booklet we shall first examine the biblical teaching concerning divine omniscience and, in particular, God's knowledge of future contingents—a chapter which is relatively easy to digest.  We shall then explore in some depth philosophical grounds for affirming divine foreknowledge of future contingents.  Two objections commonly lodged by Openness theologians against divine foreknowledge shall then be taken up and assessed.  Finally, we shall consider the powerful but somewhat controversial doctrine known as divine middle knowledge.

These topics are not easy ones, but they are important ones.  How we come down with respect to these questions will lead to radically different concepts of God.  Options must not be embraced rashly or whimsically.  They must be pondered long and hard.

# THE BIBLICAL DOCTRINE OF DIVINE FOREKNOWLEDGE

## ♆ Chapter 1 ♅

The suggestion on the part of Openness theologians that the God described in the Bible is ignorant of future contingents is on the face of it an extraordinary claim. For not only are the Scriptures replete with examples of precisely such knowledge on God's part, but they explicitly teach that God has foreknowledge of future events, even employing a specialist vocabulary to refer to such knowledge. The New Testament introduces a whole family of words associated with God's knowledge of the future, such as "foreknow" (*proginōskō*), "foreknowledge" (*prognōsis*), "foresee" (*prooraō*), "foreordain" (*proorizō*), and "foretell" (*promarturomai, prokatangellō*). Thus, the claim that the biblical concept of omniscience does not include knowledge of the future seems quite surprising.

The biblical affirmation of God's knowledge of the future is important in two respects. *First, this aspect of divine omniscience underlies the biblical scheme of history.* For the biblical conception of history is not the idea of an unpredictably unfolding sequence of events plunging haphazardly without purpose or direction; rather, God knows the future and directs the course of world history toward His foreseen ends:

> I am God, and there is none like me,
> declaring the end from the beginning
> and from ancient times things not yet done,
> saying, "My counsel shall stand,
> and I will accomplish all my purpose."
> (Isa. 46:9-10)[1]

Biblical history is a salvation history, and Christ is the beginning, centerpiece, and culmination of that history. God's plan of salvation was not an afterthought necessitated by an unforeseen circumstance. Paul speaks of "the plan of the mystery hidden for ages in God, who created all things," "a plan for the fullness of time" according to "the eternal purpose which he has realized in Christ Jesus our Lord" (Eph. 3:9; 1:10; 3:11; cf. 2 Tim. 1:9-10). Similarly, Peter states that Christ's death "was destined before the foundation of the world but was made manifest at the end of the times for your sake" (1 Peter 1:20). Indeed, it would be wrong-headed for biblical writers to speak of God's plan of salvation from "before the foundations of the earth" if God did not even know whether the first human beings would rebel against Him! God's knowledge of the course of world history and His control over it to achieve His purposes are fundamental to the biblical conception of history and are a source of comfort and assurance to the believer in times of distress.

Second, *God's knowledge of the future—including the future free choices of humans—seems essential to the prophetic pattern that underlies the biblical scheme of history.* The test of the true prophet was success in foretelling the future: "When a prophet speaks in the name of the Lord, if the word does not come to pass or come true, that is a word which the Lord has not spoken" (Deut. 18:22). The history of Israel was punctuated with prophets who foretold events in both the immediate and distant future, and it was the conviction of the New Testament writers that the coming and work of Jesus had been prophesied.

The prophetic element, however, is not limited to the fulfillment of Old Testament predictions. Jesus himself is characterized as a prophet, and he predicts his own execution, the destruction of Jerusalem, signs of the end of the world, and his own return as Lord of all nations (Lk. 9:22; Matt. 24; Mk. 13; Lk. 21). In the early church, too, there were prophets who told of events to come (Acts 11:27-28; 21:10-11; see also 13:1; 15:32; 21:9; 1 Cor. 12:28-29; 14:29, 37; Eph. 4:11). The Revelation to John is a mighty vision of the end of human history: "The Lord, the God of the spirits of the prophets, has sent his angel to show his servants what must soon take place" (Rev. 22:6). The prophetic pattern thus reveals an underlying unity, not only between the two Testaments, but beneath the entire course of human history.

The biblical view of history and prophecy thus seems to necessitate a God who knows not only the present and past, but also the future. Indeed, so essential is God's knowledge of the future that Isaiah makes knowledge of the future the decisive test in distinguishing the true God from false gods. The prophet flings this challenge in the teeth of all pretenders to deity:

> "Set forth your case," says the Lord;
> "bring your proofs," says the King of Jacob.
> "Let them bring them, and tell us
> what is to happen.
> Tell us the former things, what they are,
> that we may consider them,
> that we may know their outcome;
> or declare to us the things to come.
> Tell us what is to come hereafter,
> that we may know that you are gods;
> do good, or do harm,
> that we may be dismayed and terrified.
> Behold, you are nothing,
> and your work is less than nothing;
> an abomination is he who chooses you."
> (Isa. 41:21-24)

Stephen Charnock (1628-1680) in his classic *Existence and Attributes of God* comments on this passage:

> Such a foreknowledge of things to come is here ascribed to God by God himself, as a distinction of him from all false Gods. Such a knowledge that, if any could prove that they were possessors of, he would acknowledge them as Gods as well as himself: "that we may know that you are Gods." He puts his Deity to stand or fall upon this account, and this should be the point which should decide the controversy whether he or the heathen idols were the true God. The dispute is managed by this

medium: he that knows things to come is God; I know things to come, *ergo* I am God: the idols know not things to come, therefore they are not Gods. God submits the being of his Deity to this trial. If God knows things to come no more than the heathen idols, which were either devils or men, he would be, in his own account, no more a God than devils or men . . . It cannot be understood of future things in their causes, when the effects necessarily arise from such causes, as light from the sun and heat from the fire. Many of these men know; more of them, angels and devils know; if God, therefore, had not a higher and farther knowledge than this, he would not by this be proved to be God, any more than angels and devils, who know necessary effects in their causes. The devils, indeed, did predict some things in the heathen oracles, but God is differenced from them here . . . in being able to predict things to come that they knew not, or things in their particularities, things that depended on the liberty of man's will, which the devils could lay no claim to a certain knowledge of. Were it only a conjectural knowledge that is here meant, the devils might answer they can conjecture, and so their deity were as good as God's . . . . God asserts his knowledge of things to come as a manifest evidence of his Godhead; those that deny, therefore, the argument that proves it, deny the conclusion, too; for this will necessarily follow, that if he be God because he knows future things, then he that doth not know future things is not God; and if God knows not future things but only by conjecture, then there is no God, because a certain knowledge, so as infallibly to predict things to come, is an inseparable perfection of the Deity.[2]

As Charnock notes, God's knowledge must encompass future contingents. Just as God knows the thoughts humans presently have, so he foreknows the very thoughts they will have.

The psalmist declares,

> O Lord, you have searched me and known me!
> You know when I sit down and when I rise up;
> you discern my thoughts from afar.
> You search out my path and my lying down
> and are acquainted with all my ways.
> Even before a word is on my tongue,
> behold, O Lord, you know it altogether.
> You hem me in, behind and before,
> and lay your hand upon me.
> Such knowledge is too wonderful for me;
> it is high; I cannot attain it.
>
> (Ps. 139:1-6)

Here the psalmist envisages himself as surrounded by God's knowledge. God knows everything about him, even his thoughts. "From afar" (*merahoq*) may be taken to indicate temporal distance—God knows the psalmist's thoughts long before he thinks them. Similarly, even before he speaks a word, God knows what he will say. Little wonder that such knowledge is beyond the reach of the psalmist's understanding! But such is the knowledge of Israel's God in contradistinction to all the false gods of her neighbors. *The God of Israel was conceived to possess foreknowledge of the future, a property which distinguished Him from all false gods.*

Moreover, the Scriptures make it clear that God also has hypothetical knowledge of conditional future contingents; that is to say, He knows what would happen if human beings were to make some free choice in a particular set of circumstances. Such knowledge is even more remarkable than simple foreknowledge, for in the case of foreknowledge the events foreknown actually do happen, whereas in the case of hypothetical knowledge, God knows what people would freely do under various circumstances whether the events ever happen or not. One of the classic examples of such hypothetical knowledge on God's part is found in I Samuel 23:6-10, which tells of David's inquiry of the Lord by means of a divining device called an ephod. David asks the Lord whether King Saul will attack the city of Keilah, where David is holed up, and whether the men of Keilah will deliver David over to Saul. In both cases, the device (which apparently gave either a "yes" or "no" answer) registers an affirmative response. And thus David flees the city so that the predictions do not in fact come true. What the device had mediated to David was not, therefore, simple foreknowledge ("Saul/the men of Kielah *will do* X"), but hypothetical knowledge ("*If* David stays, then Saul/the men of Kielah *will do* X"). God was letting David know that if he *were* to remain at Keilah, then Saul *would* come after him and that if Saul *were* to come after David, then the men of Keilah *would* deliver him over to Saul. By acting on such knowledge, David was able to save his life and those of his men. The answers given by the divining device were thus correct answers, even though the events did not come to pass, since the answers were indicative of what would happen under certain circumstances.

Although most Scriptural prophecy is given in an unconditional way, sometimes prophecies are provided explicitly in the conditional form that David received at Keilah. Consider, for example, Jeremiah's prophecy to King Zedekiah:

> "Thus says the Lord, the God of hosts, the God of Israel: If you will surrender to the officials of the king of Babylon, then your life shall be spared, and this city shall not be burned with fire, and you and your house shall live. But if you do not surrender to the officials of the king of Babylon, then this city shall be given into the hand of the Chaldeans, and they shall burn it with fire, and you shall not escape from their hand" (Jer. 38:17-18).

In His omniscience God knew what would happen whichever course of action Zedekiah chose. Indeed, construing certain prophecies as hypothetical warnings rather than as categorical declarations of simple foreknowledge enables us to explain how it is that in Israel the test of a true prophet was the fulfillment of his predictions (Deut. 18:22) and yet, some predictions given by true prophets do not actually come to pass due to a change on the part of the people forewarned

(Amos 7:1-6; Jonah 3; Isa. 38:1-5). In such cases, what God was giving was hypothetical knowledge of what would happen under the prevailing circumstances; but were intercessory prayer or repentance to occur, then God would not carry out what had been threatened.

We also find hypothetical knowledge exhibited by Christ. For example, he tells Peter, "Go to the sea and cast a hook, and take the first fish that comes up, and when you open its mouth, you will find a shekel; take that and give it to them for me and for yourself" (Matt. 17:27). The passage is most naturally understood as an expression of Jesus' knowledge that if Peter were to carry out Jesus' instructions, he would find things as the Lord predicted. Or again, Jesus commands the disciples after a futile night of fishing, "Cast the net on the right side of the boat, and you will find some [fish]" (John 21:6). The miraculous catch that ensued shows that Jesus knew exactly what would happen if the disciples obeyed his command. Sometimes Jesus makes hypothetical statements himself: "If I had not come and spoken to them, they would not have sin . . . . If I had not done among them the works which no one else did, they would not have sin" (John 15:22, 24). "If my kingdom were of this world, my servants would have been fighting, that I might not be delivered over to the Jews" (John 18:36). "Woe to that man by whom the Son of Man is betrayed! It would be better for that man if he had not been born" (Matt. 26:24). Examples of this sort could be multiplied.

It is plain, then, that the God of the Bible exhibits hypothetical knowledge. Given God's infallibility, it will not do to construe these examples as mere hunches on God's part. If God believes that Saul would besiege Keilah if David were to stay there, then that hypothetical statement is known by God to be true.

Therefore, in light of the clear biblical affirmations of divine foreknowledge and hypothetical knowledge, it might seem surprising that some conservative theologians would deny that the Bible teaches that God possesses such knowledge. Those who hold to this revisionist view, however, typically point to passages in the Scriptures which imply that God is ignorant of some fact (for example, Jer. 26:3; 36:3). Thus, He does not have complete knowledge of the future.

Now certainly there are passages which, taken at face value, seem to imply God's ignorance of certain facts. However, the whole question is how we should understand such passages. Openness theologians insist on taking such passages at face value, just as they stand. Here two problems arise.

*First, a consistent application of this naïve way of interpreting the Bible leads to a defective concept of God.* For not only are there biblical passages implying God's ignorance of future events but also of present and past events. For example, in Genesis we read the story of God's appearing to Abraham prior to His judgment upon Sodom and Gomorrah. The story recounts, "Then the Lord said, 'Because the outcry against Sodom and Gomorrah is great and their sin is grave, I will go down to see whether they have done altogether according to the outcry which has come to me; and if not, I will know'"(Gen. 18:20-21). There then follows an amusing dialogue between Abraham and God in which Abraham, like a shrewd Middle Eastern merchant, bargains God down to a minimum number of righteous persons He must find in order to preserve the cities from destruction! Taken at face value, this lively exchange implies God's ignorance, not only of future contingents, but of *past* and *present* events (" . . . .and if not, I will know . . . .") which any *human* observer could have known. Or again, in the story of Abraham and Isaac, God's tests Abraham's faith by commanding him to slay his son. Before Abraham can carry out the deed, God halts him mid-course, saying, "Now I know that you fear God, seeing that you have not withheld your son, your only son, from me" (Gen. 22.12). Taken at face value, the story implies not only God's ignorance of the future but also of the present state of Abraham's heart and the depth of his commitment ("Now I know"). Thus, a consistent application of the naïve hermeneutic of Openness theologians leads to a cognitively limited deity who is ignorant not only of the future but also the past and present.

It gets worse. For it is striking how similar Openness theologians' naïve literalism is to that of Mormon theologians, who employ it to justify their belief in a God who is not only ignorant of future contingents but is a physical being with human form spatially located somewhere in the universe. Like Openness theologians, Mormon theologians insist on taking the biblical descriptions of God at face value and going no further. The Scripture says that God was walking in the cool of the garden (Gen. 3:8). Walking necessitates having legs. The Scriptures describe God as having eyes and ears and arms and hands. What could be clearer than that God has a finite, humanoid body? Openness theologians would doubtless respond that these descriptions must be taken as metaphors, since we have other passages in Scripture asserting the spirituality and omnipresence of God. But a Mormon theologian like Stephen Robinson will happily concede the point. The fact that God has a spiritual nature that is everywhere present, he insists, does not refute the clear affirmation of Scripture that He also has a physical nature which is spatially circumscribed. What is awkward for Openness theologians is that there are far more passages implying divine corporeality (God as embodied or physical) than divine ignorance of future contingents, and fewer passages affirming divine incorporeality than divine foreknowledge. It is difficult to see how one can adopt Openness theologians' naïve literalism with respect to divine knowledge and yet reject it with respect to divine corporeality. Mormon theologians realize this and have therefore warmly embraced Openness theologians.

That leads to the second point. The fundamental flaw of this naïve hermeneutic is its failure to appreciate that *the Bible is not a textbook in systematic theology or philosophy of religion but is largely a collection of stories about God's dealings with human beings.* These stories are told from the human perspective and evince all the liveliness of the storyteller's art. The storyteller's task is not to reflect philosophically upon his narrative but to offer a vivid description. Thus, the Scriptures are filled with anthropomorphisms, that is to say, descriptions of God in human terms—many so subtle that they escape our notice. There are not only the obvious anthropomorphisms, such as references to God's eyes, hands, and nostrils, but almost unconscious anthropomorphisms, such as references to God's seeing the distress of His people, hearing their prayers, crushing His enemies, turning away from apostate Israel, and so forth. These are all *metaphors*, since God does not possess literal bodily parts by which to accomplish these actions. In the same way, given the explicit teaching of Scripture that God does foreknow the future, the passages that portray God as ignorant or inquiring are plausibly to be understood as anthropomorphisms characteristic of the genre of narrative. Contrary to Openness theologians, we have every reason to be suspicious of a literal interpretation of passages that portray God as finite or limited.

Those who deny divine foreknowledge also appeal to passages in which God predicts that something will happen, but then "repents," so that the predicted event does not come to pass (e.g., Amos 7:1-6; Jon. 3; Isa. 38:1-5). Obviously, since what God predicted did not in the end happen, the predictions were not foreknowledge of the future. The problem here is to explain how the authors of such passages could affirm that God knows the future and cannot lie (Num. 23:19; 1 Sam. 15:29) and yet could represent Him as relenting on impending judgments that He had commanded His prophets to proclaim.

Such passages are plausibly interpreted as anthropomorphic narratives portraying God's hypothetical knowledge of conditional future contingents. In general, the truth communicated to us by these passages is that God's sovereignty does not consist of blind decrees operating irrespective of free human responses. These passages require that any adequate account of divine sovereignty make adequate room for human freedom. God's sovereignty takes into account and is significantly conditioned by the free acts of creatures. This truth is expressed from the human point of view in terms of God's disappointment or frustration or relenting on planned action. The most plausible interpretation of such passages, therefore, is that these prophecies were not simple glimpses of the future, but warnings of what was going to happen *unless* . . . .[3]

14

The prophecies contained the implicit condition "all things remaining the same." Certain prophecies thus are *forecasts* or *fore-warnings* of what is going to happen if all things remain as they are. Far from detracting from God's knowledge, then, such passages actually serve to enlarge it beyond knowledge of absolute future contingents (events that will happen) to conditional future contingents (events that would happen under some set of circumstances).

Not all of the prophecies in the Old and New Testaments are forewarnings, however. How do Openness theologians explain Scriptural passages which illustrate actual foreknowledge on God's part? Typically, they attempt to explain away each example of divine foreknowledge as being one of the following: (1) a *declaration* by God of what He Himself intends to bring about, (2) an *inference* of what is going to happen based on present causes, or (3) a *conditional prediction* of what will happen if something else happens.

Such an account seems inadequate, however. As far as (3)—*conditional prediction*—is concerned, if conditional predictions do not reduce to (1) or (2), they must be expressions of divine hypothetical knowledge, which is even more remarkable than divine foreknowledge, and, indeed, as we shall see, may even provide the basis for divine foreknowledge. Hence, to try to explain away divine foreknowledge by means of (3) is counterproductive.

As for (2)—the *inference* explanation—events such as Judas's betrayal or Peter's denials cannot have been caused by God, since they concern sinful acts, of which God cannot be the author. But neither are they plausibly determined by historical or human (secondary) causes. Any attempt to explain away Jesus' predictions of these events as inferences from the flawed character and circumstances of these men is fanciful. Granted that Jesus could infer that Peter would fail him, how could he infer that Peter's failure would come in the form of denials, rather than, say, flight, or silence, or lies, and how could he infer *three* denials on Peter's part, and that before the cock crowed *twice*?

Even more fundamentally, however, such an interpretation of these passages is theologically obtuse.

For even if it might be plausibly claimed that Jesus predicted Judas's betrayal or Peter's denials solely on the basis of their character and the surrounding circumstances, there can be no question that the Gospel writers themselves did not so understand such predictions. To try to explain such biblical prophecies as mere inferences from present states of affairs strips them of any theological significance. The writers of Scripture clearly saw prophecy not as God's educated guesswork about what might happen, but as a manifestation of His infinite knowledge, encompassing even things yet to come. Some Openness theologians have said that God, knowing the character of Judas and Peter, "orchestrated" the circumstances to lead them to do such acts, so that they were predictable. But in the absence of hypothetical knowledge, the claim that God orchestrated the circumstances to bring about Peter's three-fold denial implies that God took away the freedom of the servant girl and the soldiers and all the others in the courtyard of the high priest's house, as well as of those at the arrest of Jesus. Thus, perversely, the Openness view winds up destroying contingency and freedom—what we end up with is, in fact, the deterministic predestination which Openness theologians are at pains to avoid!

As for (1)—the *declaration of God's intentions*—it is true that many prophecies in Scripture are clearly based on God's irrevocable intention to bring about certain future events on His own. In such cases, prophecy serves to manifest not so much God's omniscience as His omnipotence, His ability to bring about whatever He intends. But the problem with (1) is that it simply cannot be stretched to cover all the cases that its proponents need it to cover. Divine foreknowledge of free human actions cannot be accounted for by (1), since it negates human freedom. Explanation (1) is useful only in accounting for God's knowledge of events which He Himself will bring about directly, not through human decisions. But Scripture provides many examples of divine foreknowledge of events which God does not directly cause, events which are the result of free human choices which God nevertheless foreknew.

In sum, prophecies of events which actually do happen and which are brought about, not by God, but by human beings and which could not have been inferred from present causes must be considered to express foreknowledge on God's part.

Finally, none of the above three explanations comes to grips with the Scriptures' *doctrinal teaching* concerning God's foreknowledge. These explanations try to account only for examples of prophecy in the Bible and say nothing about the passages which explicitly teach that God foreknows the future.

In conclusion, on the basis of our examination of the biblical text, we have found strong warrant for the doctrine that *God's omniscience encompasses all events, including knowledge of all absolute and conditional future contingents.* Biblical stories suggesting the contrary are best understood as being due to the non-systematic character of the narrative genre, which often employs anthropomorphic descriptions of God's person or activity.

# PHILOSOPHICAL GROUNDS FOR AFFIRMING DIVINE FOREKNOWLEDGE

## 𝔔 Chapter 2 𝔔

Having considered biblical grounds for affirming God's foreknowledge of future contingents, we now want to examine what philosophical reasons there might be for thinking that God knows the future. As St. Anselm (1033-1109) saw, the concept of God is the concept of a perfect being, what Anselm termed "the greatest conceivable being." (Just ask yourself whether any being which is less than perfect would be worthy of worship.) Now the greatest conceivable being, a perfect being, must be all-knowing (omniscient). For ignorance is an imperfection; all things being equal, it is greater or better to be knowing than ignorant. Therefore, if there are truths about future contingents, God, as an omniscient being, must know these truths. Since there are such truths about the future (i.e., since propositions about future contingents are either true or false, and they are not all false), God must therefore know all truths about the future (i.e., He knows everything that will happen).

It will help us keep our thinking clear if we express this reasoning in the form of several steps or premises as follows:

1. God is a perfect being.
2. Any being which is perfect is omniscient.
3. An omniscient being knows all truths.
4. There are truths about future contingents.

From these four premises we can conclude:

  5.  Therefore, God is omniscient. (from 1, 2)
  6.  Therefore, God knows all truths. (from 3, 5)
  7.  Therefore, God knows all truths about future contingents. (from 4, 6)

Let's now look at each premise in order to see why we should regard each step of the argument as true.

Premises (1) and (2) seem to be incontestable. By definition God is a being which is worthy of worship, and no imperfect being could merit such unqualified adoration. Moreover, as a perfection, omniscience would seem to be among the attributes of any perfect being. The first two steps of the argument are therefore uncontroversial.

So the Openness theologian, if he is to resist the force of this reasoning, will have to attack either premise (3) or premise (4). Unfortunately, things get pretty technical here. However, we cannot do justice to this momentous topic without going into significant detail. Furthermore, since so many Openness theologians have denied either (3) or (4), we simply cannot forego a discussion of these premises and the objections of Openness theologians to them. These two premises lie at the very heart of the debate.

Now premise (3) seems to be true by definition: to be omniscient just means to know only and all truths. Those who want to deny (3) are therefore forced to come up with a new definition of omniscience that does not involve knowledge of all truths.

Now in order to understand the concept of omniscience, we need to understand what philosophers call a proposition. A *proposition* is the *information content of a declarative sentence*. *Sentences* are thus *linguistic expressions of propositions*. For example, the English sentence "Snow is white" and the German sentence "*Der Schnee ist weiss*" both express the same proposition because they have the same information content, namely, that snow is white. Propositions, as philosophers use the term, are thus *bits of information*.

The information conveyed by a sentence can be either *true* information or *false* information.

Propositions can thus be either true or false, and we call sentences true or false based on whether they express true information or not. Some propositions may never actually be expressed linguistically in the form of sentences. For example, up to this point, the proposition that *On 1 January 2002, Ravi Zacharias climbed Mt. Everest* has probably never been expressed in a sentence before! But still that proposition provides either true information or false information. Indeed, when we reflect on the fact that there are only a finite number of language users in the world, whereas information is endless, we realize that most propositions have never been and will never be expressed in the form of actual sentences. But those propositions are still either true or false. We say that propositions thus have a truth value: either the value *true* or the value *false*.

Propositions have their truth values either necessarily or contingently. If a proposition has its truth value necessarily, then it is impossible for it to have the opposite truth value. If it is necessarily true, it is impossible for it to be false. If it is necessarily false, then it is impossible for it to be true. For example, *Everything that has a shape has a size* seems to be necessarily true, and *Something is both red all over and green all over* seems to be necessarily false. On the other hand, propositions which can have opposite truth values have their truth values only contingently. For example, *George W. Bush won the Presidential election of 2000* is only contingently true. He could have lost! So that proposition has its truth value only contingently. But there is another reason why that proposition is only contingently true. It is in the past tense. Therefore, this proposition was true only *after* the 2000 election. What was true prior to the election was the future tense proposition *George W. Bush will win the Presidential election of 2000*. When he won, that future tense proposition abruptly switched truth values. So did the past tense proposition. The former went from being true to being false, and the latter went from being false to being true. Thus, the passage of time affects the truth value of tensed propositions.

Finally, propositions are the objects of belief and knowledge. When we say that we know that snow is white, we are claiming to know, not some English *sentence*, but the *information* expressed by that sentence. Thus, a German and an American both know and believe the same thing even though one asserts, "*Der Schnee ist weiss*," and the other asserts, "Snow is white." Obviously, not all our beliefs are true. Sometimes we believe false information. In that case we believe a false proposition. But *knowledge entails true belief.* That's part of what we mean by the word "knowledge." *If you **know** something, then it is **true**.* It follows that only true propositions can be objects of knowledge. False propositions, as well as true ones, can be believed, but *only true propositions can be known* (i.e., it's impossible to *know* what is *false*).

With these preliminaries in mind, we are now ready to understand the traditional definition of omniscience. Consider any person P and any proposition *p*:

> O. P is omniscient = If *p* is true, then P knows that *p* and does not believe not-*p*.

What (O) requires is that a person is omniscient if and only if he knows all truths and believes no falsehoods. This is the standard definition of omniscience. It entails that if there are future-tense truths, then an omniscient being must know them.

Opponents of divine foreknowledge have suggested revisionary definitions of omniscience so that they can affirm that God is omniscient, even though He lacks knowledge of future contingents.[4] William Hasker's revisionist definition is typical:

> O'. God is omniscient = God knows all propositions which are such that God's knowing them is logically possible.

Revisionists then go on to claim that it is logically impossible to know propositions about future contingents, and so God may count as omniscient despite His ignorance of an infinite number of true future-tense propositions.

As it stands, however, (O′) is drastically flawed. *For it does not exclude that God believes false propositions as well as true ones.* Worse, (O′) actually *requires* God to know false propositions, which is incoherent as well as theologically unacceptable. For (O′) requires that if it is logically possible for God to know some proposition $p$, then God knows $p$. But if $p$ is a contingently false proposition, say, *There are eight planets in the solar system*, then there are possible worlds in which $p$ is true and so known by God.[5] Therefore, since it is logically possible for God to know $p$, He must according to (O′) actually know $p$, which is absurd.

Perhaps we can help the revisionist formulate his re-definition more adequately. What the revisionist really wants to say is something like

> O″. God is omniscient = God knows only and all true propositions which are such that it is logically possible for God to know them.

The difference in this definition is that by adding the qualifying phrase "only and all true propositions," it stipulates that the scope of God's knowledge is restricted to true propositions. Unlike (O′), (O″) limits God's knowledge to a certain subset of all true propositions, namely, those which it is logically possible for God to know.

The fundamental problem with all such revisionary definitions of omniscience as (O″) is that *any adequate definition of a concept must accord with our intuitive understanding of the concept.* We are not at liberty to "cook" a definition in some desired way without thereby making the definition unacceptably contrived. (O″) is guilty of being "cooked" in this way. For, intuitively, omniscience involves knowing all truths, yet according to (O″) God could conceivably be ignorant of infinite realms of truths and yet still count as "omniscient." The only reason why someone would prefer (O″) to (O) is due to an ulterior motivation to salvage the attribute of omniscience for a cognitively limited deity rather than to deny outright that God is omniscient. (O″) is therefore unacceptably contrived.

A second problem with (O″) is that it construes omniscience in *modal*—rather than *categorical*—terms.[6] That is, it speaks, not of knowing all truth (*categorical*), but of knowing all truth that is knowable (*modal*). But omniscience, unlike omnipotence, is not a modal notion. Roughly speaking, omnipotence is the capability of bringing about any logically possible (modal) state of affairs. But omniscience is not merely the *capability* of knowing only and all truths; it *is* knowing only and all truths (categorical). Nor does omniscience mean knowing only and all knowable truths, but knowing only and all truths, period. It is a categorical, not a modal, notion.

Third, the superiority of (O″) over (O) depends on there being an intrinsic difference between *a truth* and *a truth which it is logically possible to know*. If there is no difference, then (O″) collapses back to (O), and the revisionist has gained nothing. But it is far from evident that there is any intrinsic difference. For what is a sufficient condition for a proposition to be logically knowable? So far as I can see, the only condition is that the proposition be true. What more is needed? If the revisionist thinks that something more is needed, then we may ask him for an example of a proposition that could be true but logically impossible to know. A proposition like *Nothing exists* or *All persons have ceased to exist* comes to mind. If these were true, they could not possibly be known to be true. But on traditional theism these propositions are necessarily false, since God is a personal being whose non-existence is impossible. *Unless the revisionist can give us some reason to think that a proposition can be true and yet unknowable, we have no reason to adopt (O″).* It seems that the only intrinsic property which a proposition must possess in order to be logically knowable is *truth*.

The revisionist will no doubt claim at this point that propositions about future contingents are logically impossible for God to know. For if He knows them, then they are necessarily true, not contingently true. This is an assertion of *theological fatalism*, the doctrine that if God knows some future-tense proposition *p*, then *p* is necessarily true. We shall examine the fatalist's argument below; but here we may note that even if we concede that his argument is sound, it still does not follow that future contingent propositions are logically impossible for God to know. The revisionist claims that for any future-tense proposition $p$, it is impossible that God know $p$ and $p$ be contingently true. Therefore, he reasons, if $p$ is contingently true, it is not possible that God knows $p$. Thus, by his revised definition of omniscience, God is exempted from having to know $p$.

But such reasoning is logically fallacious. The fallacy in this reasoning can be exposed as follows. The two premises

> A.  Not-possibly (God knows $p$, and $p$ is contingently true)

and

> B.  $p$ is contingently true

do not logically entail that

> C.  Not-possibly (God knows $p$)

This is just a logically invalid inference. It violates the rules of logic. Rather, what follows logically from (A) and (B) is merely

> C'.  Not (God knows $p$).

In other words, what follows from (A) and (B) is merely that God does not know $p$, not that it is *impossible* that God knows $p$.

Thus, even *granted* the fatalist's premise (A) that it is impossible that God know $p$ and $p$ be contingently true, it does not follow from the contingency of $p$ that $p$ is such that it is logically impossible for God to know $p$. Therefore, even on the defective definition (O″) proposed by the revisionist, *the revisionist's God turns out not to be omniscient*, since $p$ is a true proposition which, so far as we can see, is logically possible for God to know, and yet God does *not* know $p$. Thus, the revisionist must deny divine omniscience and therefore reject God's perfection—a very serious theological consequence indeed![7]

So Openness theologians have no choice in the end but to deny

4. There are truths about future contingents.

That is to say, they must deny that any future-tense, contingent propositions have the truth value *true*.

How can this be done? Openness theologians might try to deny the truth of future contingent propositions by *contending that such propositions are neither true nor false*. They, in effect, have no truth value. Such a view cannot, however, be plausibly maintained.

First, *there is no good reason to think that future-tense propositions are neither true nor false*. Why should we accept the view that future-tense propositions about free acts—propositions which we use all the time in ordinary conversation and, moreover, are found in Scripture—are in fact neither true nor false? What proof is there that such propositions are neither true nor false?

About the only answer of any substance ever given to this question goes something like this: "Future events, unlike present events, do not exist. Now, a proposition is true if and only if it corresponds to what exists, and false if and only if it does not correspond to what exists. Since the future does not exist, there is nothing for future-tense propositions to correspond with or to fail to correspond with. Hence, future-tense propositions cannot be true or false."

Such an argument presupposes a view of time according to which the past, present, and future are not equally real. Although such a view is controversial, still it seems plausible; so let us assume that this view is correct. The issue is then whether, given such a view of time, the definition of truth as correspondence requires us to deny that future-tense propositions are either true or false. Those who think so seem to misunderstand the concept of truth as correspondence. A view of truth as correspondence holds merely that a proposition is true if and only if what it states to be the case really is the case. For example, the proposition *It is snowing* is true if and only if it is snowing. Although this might seem too obvious to be worth stating, it is sometimes misunderstood.

*Truth as correspondence does not mean that the things or events which a true proposition is about must (now) exist.* Indeed, it is only in the case of true *present-tense* propositions that the things or events referred to must *(now) exist.* For a *past*-tense proposition to be true, it is not required that what it describes exist in the present, but only that it *have* existed. For a *future*-tense proposition to be true, it is not required that what it describes exist now, but that it *will* exist. In order for a future-tense proposition to be true, all that is required is that when the moment described arrives, the present-tense version of the proposition will be true. The idea that the concept of truth as correspondence requires that the things or events described by the proposition must exist at the time the proposition is true is a complete misunderstanding.

To say that a future-tense proposition is now true is not, of course, to say that we may now *know* whether it is true or to say that things are now so *determined* that it is true. It is only to say that *when the time arrives, things will turn out as the proposition predicts. A future-tense proposition is true if matters turn out as the proposition predicts, and false if matters fail to turn out as the proposition predicts—this is all that the notion of truth as correspondence requires.* Hence, there is no good reason to deny that future-tense propositions are either true or false.

Second, *there are several good reasons to maintain that future-tense propositions are either true or false.*

(i) The same facts that guarantee the truth or falsity of present- and past-tense propositions also guarantee the truth or falsity of future-tense propositions. Nicholas Rescher explains,

Difficulties about divine foreknowledge quite apart, it is difficult to justify granting to
1. "It will rain tomorrow" (asserted on April 12)
a truth status different from that of

2. "It did rain yesterday" (asserted on April 14) because both make (from temporally distinct perspectives) *precisely the same claim about the facts,* viz., rain on April 13.[8]

Think about it for a moment. If *It is raining today* is now true, how could *It will rain tomorrow* not have been true yesterday? The same facts guarantee that a future-tense proposition *asserted earlier*, a present-tense proposition *asserted simultaneously*, and a past-tense proposition *asserted later* are all true.

(ii) If *future-tense propositions are not true, then neither are past-tense propositions.* If future-tense propositions cannot be true because the realities they describe do not yet exist, then by the same token past-tense propositions cannot be true because the realities they describe no longer exist. But to maintain that past-tense propositions cannot be true would be ridiculous. Since the two cases are parallel, one must either deny the truth or falsity of both past- and future-tense propositions or affirm the truth or falsity of both.

(iii) *Tenseless propositions are always true or false.* It is possible to eliminate the tense of the verb expressed in a proposition by specifying the time at which the proposition is supposed to be true. For example, the proposition *The Allies invaded Normandy* can be made tenseless by specifying the time: *On 6 June 1944, the Allies invade Normandy,* the verb "invade" being tenseless. If the tensed version is true, then so is the tenseless version. Thus, correlated with any true past- or present-tense proposition is a true tenseless version of that proposition. Furthermore, *a tenseless proposition, if it is true at all, is always true.* This is precisely because the proposition is tenseless. If *On 6 June 1944, the Allies invade Normandy* is *ever* true, then it is *always* true. Therefore, this proposition is true prior to June 6, 1944. But in that case, it is true prior to 6 June 1944 that the Allies on that date will invade Normandy, which is the same as saying that the future-tense version of the tenseless proposition is true. Moreover, since God is omniscient, He must always know the truth of the tenseless proposition, a fact which entails that He foreknows the future.

Third, *the denial of the truth or falsity of future-tense propositions has absurd consequences.* For example, if future-tense propositions are neither true nor false, the assertion made in 2002 "George W. Bush either will or will not win the presidential election in 2004" would not be true. For this proposition is a compound constructed from two simple future-tense sentences— "George W. Bush will win the presidential election in 2004" and "George W. Bush will not win the presidential election in 2004." If neither of these individual statements is true or false, the compound statement combining them is also neither true nor false. *But how can this be? Either Bush will win or he will not—there is no other alternative!* But the view that future-tense propositions are neither true nor false would require us to say that this compound statement is neither true nor false, which seems absurd.

Worse still, if future-tense propositions are neither true nor false, it would be impossible for us to say that a statement made in 2002 like "Bush will both win and not win the presidential election in 2004" is false. For this is a compound statement consisting of two simple future-tense statements, neither of which is supposed to be true or false. Therefore, the compound statement cannot be true or false either. But surely this statement is false, for it is a self-contradiction: Bush cannot both win and not win the election!

We must conclude that (a) with no good reason in favor of it, (b) persuasive reasons against it, and (c) absurd consequences following from it, the view that future-tense propositions about contingent events are neither true nor false is untenable. Premise (4) cannot be plausibly denied.

All the premises of our philosophical argument are therefore more plausibly true than their denials. It follows that the Openness view that God does not possess foreknowledge of future free events is untenable. As an omniscient being, God must know all true propositions, including future contingent propositions. He therefore knows the future.

# PHILOSOPHICAL OBJECTIONS TO DIVINE FOREKNOWLEDGE

## 𝕽 Chapter 3 𝕾

Opponents of the biblical doctrine of divine foreknowledge usually raise two objections to that doctrine:  (1) Divine foreknowledge is incompatible with future contingents, and  (2) There is no basis on which God can know future contingents.  Let us explore each of these issues in turn.

### THE COMPATIBILITY OF DIVINE FOREKNOWLEDGE AND FUTURE CONTINGENTS

It is clearly not biblical exegesis that is the motivating force behind Openness theologians' denial of divine foreknowledge of future contingents.  Rather the driving force behind Openness theology is *a philosophical argument derived from ancient Greek fatalism and dressed in theological guise,* and biblical exegesis is being bent to support a conclusion already determined by philosophical considerations.  Fatalism is the doctrine that everything we do we do necessarily and that therefore human freedom is an illusion.  It is alleged that if God foreknows the future, then fatalism is true.  Since fatalism is not true, it follows that God must not foreknow the future.

It is ironic that Openness theologians should appeal to such reasoning, since it is these same theologians who loudly decry the polluting influence of Greek philosophical thought upon the biblical tradition.  In fact, it seems that *it is they themselves who have been seduced by reasoning of Greek philosophical origin*—fatalistic reasoning which was stoutly resisted by the early Church Fathers.  If Openness theologians find the suggested solutions to fatalism unconvincing, then it is the better part of intellectual humility to simply confess that one lacks the philosophical insight to solve the problem (cf. Ps. 139:6) and to hold the biblical doctrines in tension rather than to deny the Scripture's clear teaching that God does know the future.

What is the argument that allegedly demonstrates the connection between divine foreknowledge and fatalism? Letting "*x*" stand for any event, the basic form of the argument is as follows:

A. Necessarily, if God foreknows $x$, then $x$ will happen.

B. God foreknows $x$.

C. Therefore, $x$ will necessarily happen.

Since $x$ happens necessarily, it is not a contingent event. In virtue of God's foreknowledge everything is fated to occur.

The problem with the above form of the argument is that it is just logically fallacious. What is validly implied by premises (A) and (B) is not (C) but

C′. Therefore, $x$ will happen.

The fatalist gets things all mixed up here. It is correct that in a sound, deductive argument the premises necessarily imply the conclusion, and the conclusion follows necessarily from the premises. That is to say, it is impossible for the premises to be true and the conclusion to be false. But *the conclusion itself need not be necessary.* The fatalist illegitimately transfers the necessity of the *inference* to the conclusion *itself.* What necessarily follows from (A) and (B) is just (C′). But the fatalist in his confusion thinks that the conclusion is itself necessarily true and so winds up with (C). In so doing he simply commits a common logical fallacy.

The correct conclusion (C′) is in no way incompatible with human freedom. From God's knowledge that I **shall** do $x$, it does *not* follow that I **must** do $x$ but only that I **shall** do $x$. God's knowing

30

that I shall do something freely is far different from the notion that I must do it. God's knowledge is in no way incompatible with my doing $x$ freely.

Undoubtedly a major source of the fatalist's confusion is his blurring together *certainty* with *necessity*.  One frequently finds in the writings of contemporary theological fatalists statements which slide from affirming that something is *certainly* true to affirming that it is *necessarily* true.  This is sheer confusion. *Certainty is a property of **persons** and has nothing to do with **truth***, as is evident from the fact that we can be absolutely certain about something which turns out to be false.  By contrast, *necessity is a property of **propositions***, indicating that a true proposition cannot possibly be false.  We can be wholly uncertain about propositions that are, unbeknownst to us, necessarily true (imagine some complex mathematical equation or theorem).  Thus, when we say that some proposition is "certainly true," this is but a manner of speaking indicating that we feel certain that the proposition is true. *People are certain* (in their thinking); *propositions are necessary* (in their truth value).

By confusing certainty and necessity, the fatalist makes his logically fallacious argument deceptively appealing.  For it is correct that from premises (A) and (B), we can be absolutely certain that $x$ will come to pass.  But it is muddle-headed to think that because $x$ will *certainly* happen, $x$ will *necessarily* happen.  We can be certain, given God's foreknowledge, that $x$ will not fail to happen, even though it is entirely possible that $x$ fail to happen. $X$ could fail to occur, but God knows that it will not.  Therefore, we can be sure that it will happen—and happen contingently.

Contemporary theological fatalists recognize the fallaciousness of the above form of the argument and therefore try to remedy the defect by making premise (B) also necessarily true:

A.  Necessarily, if God foreknows $x$, then $x$ will happen.

B′.  Necessarily, God foreknows $x$.

C. Therefore, $x$ will necessarily happen.

So formulated, the argument is no longer logically fallacious, and so the question becomes whether the premises are true.

Premise (A) is clearly true. It is perhaps worth noting that this is the case, not because of God's essential omniscience or inerrancy, but simply in virtue of the definition of "knowledge." Since knowledge entails true belief, anybody's knowing that $x$ will happen necessarily implies that $x$ will happen. Thus, we could replace (A) and (B′) with

A.* Necessarily, if Smith correctly believes that $x$ will happen, then $x$ will happen.

B.* Necessarily, Smith correctly believes that $x$ will happen.

And (C) will follow as before. Therefore, if any person ever holds true beliefs about the future (and surely we do, as we smugly remind others when we say, "I told you so!"), then, given the truth of premise (B*), fatalism follows from merely human beliefs—a curious conclusion!

Indeed, as ancient Greek fatalists realized, *the presence of any agent at all—including God Himself—is really unnecessary to the argument.* All one needs is a true, future-tense proposition to get the argument going. Thus, we could replace (A) and (B′) with

A.** Necessarily, if it is true that $x$ will happen, then $x$ will happen.

B.** Necessarily, it is true that $x$ will happen.

And we shall get (C) as our conclusion. Thus, philosopher Susan Haack quite rightly calls the argument for theological fatalism "a needlessly (and confusingly) elaborated version" of Greek fatalism; the addition of an omniscient God to the argument constitutes a "gratuitous detour" around the real issue—namely, the truth or falsity of future-tense propositions.[9] That is, *if an event is going to happen in the future* ("It is true that *x* will happen,"), *God's omniscience is irrelevant to the matter.*

In order to avoid the above generalization of their argument to all persons and to mere propositions about the future, theological fatalists will deny that the second premise is true with respect to humans or mere propositions, as it is for God. They will say that Smith's holding a true belief or some future-tense proposition's being true are not necessary in the way that God's holding a belief is necessary.

That raises the question as to whether premise (B′) is true. Now at face value, premise (B′) seems obviously false. Christian theology has always maintained that God's creation of the world is a free act, that God could have created a different world, in which *x* does not occur, or even no world at all. To say that God necessarily foreknows any event *x* implies that this is the only world God could have created and thus denies divine freedom.

But theological fatalists have a different sort of necessity in mind when they say that God's foreknowledge is necessary. What they are talking about is *temporal necessity,* or the necessity of the past. Often this is expressed by saying that the past is unpreventible or unchangeable. If some event is in the past, then it is now too late to do anything to affect it. It is in *that* sense necessary. Since God's foreknowledge of future events is now part of the past, it is now fixed and unalterable. Therefore, given God's free creation of this particular world, it is said, premise (B′) is true.

But if premise (B′) is true in that sense, then why are not (B*) and (B**) true as well? The theological fatalist will respond that Smith's belief's being true or a future-tense proposition's being true are not facts or events of the past, as is God's holding a belief about something.

But such an understanding of what constitutes a fact or event seems quite counter-intuitive. If Smith believed in 1997 that *Clinton will be impeached,* Smith held a true belief at that time. So was it not a fact that Smith's belief was true? If Smith still held that same belief today (viz., *Clinton will be impeached*), would it not be a fact that Smith's belief is no longer true (since

Clinton's term of office is past)? If Smith's belief thus changes from being true to being false, then surely it was a fact that his belief was then true and it is a fact that his belief is now false. The same obviously goes for the mere proposition *Clinton will be impeached.* This proposition once had the property of being true and now has the property of being false. In any reasonable sense of "fact," these are past and present facts.

Indeed, a proposition's having a truth value is plausibly an event as well. This is most obvious with respect to propositions like *Flight 4750 to Paris will depart in five minutes.* That proposition is false up until five minutes prior to departure, becomes true at five minutes till, and then becomes false again immediately thereafter. Other propositions being true may be more long-lasting events, like *Flight 4750 to Paris will depart within the next hour.* Such propositions' being true are clearly events on any reasonable construal of what constitutes an event.

Theological fatalists have not even begun to address the question of the nature of facts or events in order to make it plausible that Smith's correctly believing a future-tense proposition and a future-tense proposition's being true do not count as past facts or events. But then we see that theological fatalism is not inherently theological at all. If the theological fatalist's reasoning is correct, it can be generalized to show that every time we hold a true belief about the future or even make a statement about the future that is true, then the future is fated to occur—surely an incredible inference!

Moreover, we have the best of reasons for thinking that premise (B') is defective in some way—namely, *fatalism posits a constraint on human freedom which is unintelligible.* For the fatalist admits that the events foreknown by God may be causally indeterminate; indeed, they could theoretically be completely uncaused, spontaneous events. Nevertheless, such events are said to be somehow constrained. But by what? Fate? What is that but a mere name? *If my action is causally free, how can it be constrained by the mere fact of God's knowing about it?*

Sometimes fatalists say that God's foreknowledge places a sort of logical constraint on my action. Even though I am causally free to refrain from my action, there is some sort of logical constraint upon me, rendering it impossible for me to refrain. But insofar as we can make sense of logical constraints, they are not analogous to the sort of necessitation imagined by the theological fatalist. For example, given the fact that Jones has already played basketball at least once in his life, it is now impossible for him to play basketball for the first time. He is thus not free to go out and play basketball for the first time. But *this sort of constraint is not at all analogous to theological fatalism.* For in the case we are envisioning, it is within Jones's power to play basketball or not. Whether he has played before or not, he can freely execute the actions of playing basketball. It's just that if he has played before, his actions will not *count* as playing for the first time. By contrast, the fatalist imagines that if God knows that Jones will not play basketball, then even though Jones is causally free, his actions are mysteriously constrained so that he is literally unable to walk out onto the court, dribble, and shoot. But such non-causal determinism is utterly unclear and unintelligible.

The argument for fatalism therefore must be unsound. Since premise (A) is clearly true, the trouble must lie with premise (B'). And premise (B') is notoriously problematic. For the notion of temporal necessity appealed to by the fatalist is so obscure a concept that (B') becomes a veritable mare's nest of philosophical difficulties. For example, since the necessity of premise (A) is logical necessity and the necessity of premise (B') is temporal necessity, why think that such mixing of different kinds of modality is valid? If the fatalist answers that logical necessity entails temporal necessity, so that premise (A) can be construed merely in terms of temporal necessity, then how do we know that such necessity is passed on from the premises to the conclusion, in the way that logical necessity is? Indeed, since $x$ is supposed to be a future event, how *could* it be temporally necessary? Since $x$ is neither present nor past but has yet to occur, it could not possibly be characterized by the temporal necessity supposedly inherent in past events once they have occurred. Thus, we have every reason to think that temporal necessity is not transitive. (The necessity of past events is thus not handed on to future events. For example, the necessity of God's past beliefs isn't transferred to the future events He foreknows.)

And even if this peculiar sort of necessity were transitive and so $x$ is temporally necessary, how do we know that this sort of necessity is incompatible with an action's being free? It is plausible that so long as a person's choice is causally undetermined, it is a free choice even if he is unable to choose the opposite of that choice.[10] Imagine a man with electrodes secretly implanted in his brain who is presented with the choice of doing either X or Y. The electrodes are inactive so long as the man chooses X; but if he were going to choose Y, then the electrodes would switch on and force him to choose X. If the electrodes fire, causing him to choose X, his choice of X is clearly not a free choice. But suppose that the man really wants to do X and chooses it without being causally determined to do so. In that case his choosing X is entirely free, since the electrodes do not function at all and so have no effect on his choice of X, even though the man is literally unable to choose Y. *What makes his choice free is the absence of any causally determining factors of his choosing X.* This conception of libertarian freedom has the advantage of explaining how it is that God's choosing to do good is free, even though it is impossible for God to choose sin—namely, His choosing is undetermined by causal constraints. Thus, libertarian freedom of the will does not require the ability to choose other than as one chooses. So even if $x$ were temporally necessary, such that not-$x$ cannot occur, it is not obvious that $x$ is not freely performed or chosen.

All of the above problems arise even if we concede (B′) to be true. But why think that this premise is true? What is temporal necessity anyway, and why think that God's past beliefs are now temporally necessary? Theological fatalists have never provided an adequate account of this peculiar kind of necessity. There has yet to be an explanation of temporal necessity, according to which God's past beliefs are temporally necessary, which does not reduce to either the *unalterability* or the *causal closedness* of the past.

But interpreting the necessity of the past as its unalterability (or unchangeability or unpreventability) is clearly inadequate, since the future, by definition, is just as unalterable as the past. By definition the future is what will occur, and the past is what has occurred. To *change* the future would be to bring it about that an event which will occur will not occur, which is self-contradictory. It is purely a matter of definition that the past and future cannot be changed, and no fatalistic conclusion follows from this truth. We need not be able to change the future in order to determine the future. If our actions are freely performed, then it lies within our power to determine causally what the course of future events will be, even if we do not have the power to change the future.

The fatalist will insist that the past is necessary in the sense that we do not have a similar ability to causally determine the past. The non-fatalist may happily concede the point: backward causation is impossible. But the causal closedness of the past does not imply fatalism. For freedom to refrain from doing as God knows one will do does not involve backward causation. One may happily admit that there is nothing I can now do to cause or bring about the past. Thus, I cannot cause God to have had in the past a certain belief about my future actions. But it may well lie within my power to perform freely some action A, and if A were to occur, then the past would have been different than it in fact is. Suppose, for example, that God has always believed that in the year 2004, George W. Bush would accept his party's nomination to run for a second term. Let us suppose that up until the time arrives, Bush has the ability to accept or refuse the nomination. If he were to refuse the nomination, then God would have held a different belief than the one He has in fact held. For if Bush were to refuse the nomination, then different future-tense propositions would have been true, and God, being omniscient, would have known this. Thus, He would have had different foreknowledge than that which He in fact has. The relation between one's action and a corresponding future-tense proposition about it is *not a causal relation.* Neither is the relation between a true future-tense proposition and God's believing it a causal one. Thus, *the causal closedness of the past is irrelevant.* If temporal necessity is merely the causal closedness of the past, then it is insufficient to support fatalism.

*No fatalist has set forth a conception of temporal necessity that does not amount to either the unalterability or the causal closedness of the past.* Typically, fatalists just appeal gratuitously to some sort of "Fixed Past Principle" to the effect that it is not within my power to act in such a way, that if I were to do so, then the past would have been different—which begs the question. On analysis of temporal necessity that are not reducible to either the unalterability or the causal closedness of the past, God's past beliefs always turn out *not* to be temporally necessary.[11]  It is interesting that precisely parallel conclusions follow with respect to past events in cases of time travel, backward causation, precognition, and the Special Theory of Relativity, which provide intriguing analogues to God's holding beliefs about future contingents.[12]

Thus, the argument for theological fatalism is unsound. Openness theologians  must look elsewhere for philosophical support of their position, for fatalism provides no cogent basis on which to deny the biblical doctrine of divine foreknowledge of future contingents.

## The Basis of Divine Foreknowledge of Future contingents

What, then, about that second question raised concerning divine foreknowledge, the basis of God's knowledge of future contingents? Detractors of divine foreknowledge sometimes claim that because future events do not exist, they cannot be known by God. The reasoning seems to go as follows:

A. Only events which actually exist can be known by God.

B. Future events do not exist.

C. Therefore, future events cannot be known by God.

Now, as already mentioned, premise (B) is not uncontroversial. A good many physicists and philosophers of time and space argue that future events do exist. They claim that the difference between past, present, and future is merely a subjective matter of human consciousness. For the people in the year 2015 the events of that year are just as real as the events of our present are for us, and for those people, it is we who have passed away and are unreal. On such a view God transcends the four-dimensional space-time continuum, and thus all events are eternally present to Him. It is easy on such a view to understand how God could therefore know events which to us are future.

Nevertheless, such a four-dimensional view of reality does face considerable philosophical and theological objections,[13] so that premise (B) of the above argument does seem more plausibly true than its denial. So the question becomes what reason there is to think that premise (A) is true.

In assessing the question of *how God knows* which events will transpire, it is helpful to distinguish two models of divine cognition: the *perceptualist* model and the *conceptualist* (or rationalist) model. The perceptualist model construes divine knowledge on the analogy of sense perception. God "looks" and "sees" what is there. Such a model is implicitly assumed when people speak of God's "foreseeing" the future or having "foresight" of future events. The perceptualist model of divine cognition does run into real problems when it comes to God's knowledge of the future, for, since future events do not exist, there is nothing there to perceive.[14]

By contrast on a *conceptualist* model of divine knowledge, God does not acquire His knowledge of the world by anything like perception. His knowledge of the future is *not* based on His "looking" ahead and "seeing" what lies in the future (a terribly anthropomorphic notion in any case). Rather, God's knowledge is self-contained; it is more like a mind's knowledge of innate ideas. *As an omniscient being, God has essentially the property of knowing all truths; there are truths about future events; therefore, God knows all truths concerning future events.*

Now it might be asked, "But *how* can God have innate knowledge of all truths, including truths about the future?" But it is difficult to make sense of this question. The very point of calling such knowledge innate is to deny that there is any *means* by which God acquires His knowledge, indeed, that it is appropriate to speak of God's acquiring knowledge at all. Rather, *as a perfect being, the greatest conceivable being, God simply possesses essentially knowledge of only and all truths; future contingent propositions are among the truths that there are; therefore God possesses essentially knowledge of future contingents.* To ask how He can do so is just an expression of incredulity, as if one were to ask, "How can God be omnipotent?" or "How can God be morally perfect?" or "How can God be eternal?" He just is that way, and nothing more needs to be said. *So long as we are not seduced into thinking of divine foreknowledge on the model of perception, it is no longer evident why knowledge of future continent propositions should be impossible.* A conceptualist model furnishes a clear basis for God's knowledge of future contingents.

Nonetheless, there is a version of the conceptualist model appealing to God's hypothetical knowledge which does allow us to say considerably more about the basis of God's foreknowledge of future contingents. It is called *the doctrine of middle knowledge* and is so intriguing and theologically important that it deserves to be discussed separately. In the next chapter, therefore, we shall explore more deeply this fascinating theory of divine knowledge.

For the present, however, we can conclude that the theological fatalism which lies at the root of Openness theologians' denial of divine foreknowledge of future contingents is logically fallacious, and that so long as we construe God's knowledge along the lines of a conceptualist model of cognition, there is no reason to think that God cannot have knowledge of future contingents. The objections of Openness theology to the traditional understanding of divine omniscience are therefore unsound and so fail to undermine that doctrine.

# DIVINE MIDDLE KNOWLEDGE

❧

### ❦ Chapter 4 ❦

## HISTORICAL BACKGROUND

Christian theologians have traditionally affirmed that in virtue of His omniscience God possesses what we have called hypothetical knowledge of conditional future contingents. He knows, for example, what would have happened if He had spared the Canaanites from destruction, what Napoleon would have done had he won the Battle of Waterloo, how your neighbor would respond if you were to share the Gospel with him. Not until F. D. E. Schleiermacher (1768-1834) and the advent of modern theology did theologians think to deny to God hypothetical knowledge. Everyone who considered the issue agreed that God has such knowledge.

Hypothetical knowledge is knowledge of what philosophers call counterfactual conditionals, or simply counterfactuals. *Counterfactuals are conditional statements in the subjunctive mood.* For example: "If I were rich, I would buy a Mercedes;" "If Goldwater had been elected President, he would have won the Vietnam War;" "If you were to ask her, she would say yes." Counterfactuals are so called because the antecedent ("If . . .") and/or consequent ("then . . .") clauses are typically contrary to fact: I am not rich; Goldwater was not elected President; the U.S. did not win the Vietnam War. Nevertheless, sometimes the antecedent and/or consequent are true. For example, your friend— emboldened by your assurance that "If you were to ask her, she would say yes"—does ask the girl of his dreams for a date, and she does say yes.

Counterfactual statements comprise a significant part of our ordinary language and are an indispensable part of our decision-making. "If I pulled out into traffic now, I wouldn't make it"; "If I were to ask J. B. for a raise with his mood, he'd tear my head off"; "If we sent the Third Army around the enemy's right flank, we would prevail." *Clearly life and death decisions are made daily on the basis of the presumed truth of counterfactual statements.*

Christian theologians have traditionally affirmed that God does, indeed, have knowledge of true counterfactuals and, hence, of the conditional future contingent events they describe. *What theologians did dispute, however, was, so to speak,* **when** *God has such hypothetical knowledge.* The question here did not have to do with the moment of time at which God acquired His hypothetical knowledge. For whether God is timeless or everlasting throughout time, in neither case are there truths which are unknown to God until some moment at which He discovers them. As an omniscient being, God must know every truth there is and so can never exist in a state of ignorance. Rather the "when" mentioned above refers to the point in the logical order concerning God's creative decree at which God has hypothetical knowledge.

This idea of a logical order with regard to God's decrees is a familiar one to Reformed theologians. For although all God's decrees occur at once rather than sequentially, there is a logical order among the decrees. For example, so-called *infra-lapsarians* say that God decreed Christ's death on the cross in order to remedy the fall of man into sin, so that logically God's decree of the cross comes *after* His decree of the fall. By contrast, *supra-lapsarians* say that God's primary aim for mankind was redemption via the cross, and therefore He decreed the fall in order to have something to redeem man from. On this scheme, the decree of the cross is *logically prior* to the decree of the fall. Thus, even though it was agreed on all hands that God's decrees occur all at once, nevertheless theologians debated how they were to be logically arranged.

Now a similar dispute existed among post-Reformation theologians with respect to the place of God's hypothetical knowledge. Everybody agreed that logically prior to God's decree to create a world, God has knowledge of all necessary truths, including all the possible worlds He might create. This was called

God's *natural knowledge.* It gives Him knowledge of what *could* be. Moreover, everyone agreed that logically subsequent to His decree to create a particular world, God knows all the contingent truths about the actual world, including its past, present, and future. This was called God's *free knowledge.* It involves knowledge of what *will* be. The *disputed question* was where one should place God's hypothetical knowledge of what *would* be. Is it logically prior to or posterior to the divine decree?

Catholic theologians of the Dominican order held that God's hypothetical knowledge is logically *subsequent* to His decree to create a certain world. They maintained that in decreeing that a particular world exist, God also decreed which counterfactual statements are true. Logically prior to the divine decree, there are no counterfactual truths to be known. All God knows at that logical moment is the necessary truths, including all the various possibilities.

At that logically prior moment God knows, for example, that there is a possible world in which Peter denies Christ three times and another possible world in which Peter affirms Christ, and in yet another it is Matthew who denies Christ three times, and so on. God picks one of these worlds to be actual, and thus subsequent to His decree it is true that Peter will deny Christ three times. Moreover, God knows this truth because He knows which world He has decreed. Not only so, but God in decreeing a particular world to be real also decrees which counterfactuals are true. Thus, He decrees, for example, that if Peter had instead been in such-and-such circumstances, he would have denied Christ two times. God's hypothetical knowledge, like His foreknowledge, is logically posterior to the divine creative decree.

By contrast, Catholic theologians of the Jesuit order inspired by Luis Molina (1535-1600) maintained that God's hypothetical knowledge is logically *prior* to His creative decree. This difference between the Jesuit Molinists and the Dominicans was no mere matter of theological hair-splitting! The Molinists charged that the Dominicans had in effect obliterated human freedom by making counterfactual truths a consequence of God's decree. For it is God who determines what a person would do in whatever circumstances he finds himself. By contrast, the Molinists, by placing God's hypothetical knowledge prior to the divine decree, made room for creaturely freedom by exempting counterfactual truths from God's decree. In the same way that *necessary truths* like 2+2=4 are prior to and therefore independent of God's decree, so *counterfactual truths* about how creatures would freely choose under various circumstances are prior to and independent of God's decree.

Not only does this view make room for human freedom, but it affords God a means of choosing which world of free creatures to create. For by knowing how persons would freely choose in whatever circumstances they might be in, God can, by decreeing to place just those persons in just those circumstances, bring about His ultimate purposes *through* free creaturely decisions. Thus, by employing His hypothetical knowledge, God can plan a world down to the last detail and yet do so without annihilating creaturely freedom, since what people would freely do under various circumstances is already factored into the equation by God. Since God's hypothetical knowledge lies logically in between His natural knowledge and His free knowledge, Molinists called it God's *middle knowledge.*

On the Dominican view, there is *one* logical moment prior to the divine creative decree, at which God knows the range of possible worlds which He might create, and then He chooses one of these to be actual. On the Molinist view, there are *two* logical moments prior to the divine decree: first, the moment at which He has natural knowledge of the range of possible worlds and second, the moment at which He has knowledge of the proper subset of possible worlds which, given the counterfactual propositions true at that moment, are feasible for Him to create. The counterfactuals which are true at that moment thus serve to limit the range of possible worlds to worlds feasible for God.

For example, there is a possible world in which Peter affirms Christ in precisely the same circumstances in which he in fact denied him. But given the counterfactual truth that if Peter were in precisely those circumstances he would freely deny Christ, then the possible world in which Peter freely affirms Christ in those circumstances is not feasible for God. God could *make* Peter affirm Christ in those circumstances, but then his confession would not be free.

Thus on the Molinist scheme, we have the following logical order:

Moment 1:   ...O   O   O   O   O   O...
*Natural Knowledge*:  God knows the range of **possible** worlds (what *could* be)

Moment 2:   ...      O        O   O      ...
*Middle Knowledge*:  God knows the range of **feasible** worlds (what *would* be)

---

Divine Creative Decree

---

Moment 3:                    O
*Free Knowledge*:  God knows the **actual** world (what *will* be)

## ARGUMENTS FOR MIDDLE KNOWLEDGE

Why think that the Molinist scheme is correct? Basically three lines of argument present themselves: biblical, theological, and philosophical.

### *Biblical Arguments*

Biblically speaking, it is not difficult to show that God possesses hypothetical knowledge, as we have seen. Unfortunately, this does not settle the matter of whether God has middle knowledge. For the scriptural passages show only that God possesses knowledge of counterfactual propositions, and, as I have said, until modern times all theologians agreed that God possesses such hypothetical knowledge. The question remains, *when in the logical order of things that knowledge comes: is it before or after the divine decree?* Since Scripture does not reflect upon this question, no amount of proof-texting concerning God's hypothetical knowledge can go to prove that such knowledge is *possessed logically prior to God's creative decree.* This is a matter for theological/philosophical reflection, not biblical exegesis. Thus, while it is clearly unbiblical to deny that God has simple foreknowledge and even hypothetical knowledge, those who deny middle knowledge cannot be accused of being unbiblical.

### Theological Arguments

Rather, the strongest arguments for the Molinist perspective are theological. Once one grasps the concept of middle knowledge, one will find it astonishing in its subtlety and power. Indeed, I would venture to say that it is one of the most fruitful theological concepts ever conceived. Recent studies have applied it to the issues of Christian uniqueness,[15] perseverance of the saints,[16] biblical inspiration,[17] infallibility,[18] Christology,[19] and evolutionary theory.[20] An article begs to be written on a Molinist perspective of quantum indeterminacy and divine sovereignty. With respect to the concerns of this booklet, *middle knowledge provides an illuminating account of divine foreknowledge and providence.*

We have already seen how middle knowledge can help us to understand the *basis of divine foreknowledge of future contingents.* Divine foreknowledge is based on (i) God's middle knowledge of what every creature would freely do under any circumstances and (ii) His knowledge of the divine decree to create certain sets of circumstances and to place certain creatures in them. Given middle knowledge and the divine decree, foreknowledge follows automatically as a result.

The Molinist account of *divine providence* is even more stunning than its account of divine foreknowledge. Consider the following biblical passages:

> "This Jesus, delivered up according to the definite plan and foreknowledge of God, you crucified and killed by the hands of lawless men" (Acts 2:23).

> "For truly in this city there were gathered together against your holy servant Jesus, whom you anointed, both Herod and Pontius Pilate, along with the Gentiles and the peoples of Israel, to do whatever your hand and your plan had predestined to take place" (Acts 4:27-28).

Here we have a *staggering assertion of divine sovereignty over the affairs of men*. The conspiracy to crucify Jesus, involving not only the Romans and the Jews in Jerusalem at that time, but more particularly Pilate and Herod, who tried Jesus, is said to have happened by God's plan based on His foreknowledge and fore-ordination. How are we to understand so far-reaching a providence as this?

If we take the biblical word "foreknowledge" to encompass middle knowledge, then we can make perfect sense of God's providential control over a world of free agents. For via His middle knowledge, God knew exactly which persons, if members of the Sanhedrin, would freely vote for Jesus' condemnation; which persons, if in Jerusalem, would freely demand Christ's death, favoring the release of Barabbas; what Herod, if King, would freely do in reaction to Jesus and to Pilate's plea to judge him; and what Pilate himself, if holding the prefecture of Palestine in A.D. 30, would freely do under the pressure of the Jewish leaders and the crowd. Knowing all the possible circumstances, persons, and particular arrangements of these, God decreed to create just those circumstances and just those people who would freely do what God willed to happen. Thus, the whole scenario, as Luke insists, unfolded according to *God's plan*. This is truly mind-boggling. When one reflects that the existence of the various circumstances and persons involved was itself the result of myriads of prior free choices on the part of these and other agents, and these in turn of yet other prior contingencies, and so on, then we see that *only an omniscient mind could providentially direct a world of free creatures toward His sovereignly-established ends*. In fact, Paul reflects that "None of the rulers of this age understood this, for if they had, they would not have crucified the Lord of glory" (1 Cor. 2:8). Once one grasps it, the doctrine of divine middle knowledge thus issues in adoration and praise of God for so breath-taking a sovereignty.

Now what account of divine providence can be given in the absence of middle knowledge? Advocates of divine Openness freely admit that without middle knowledge a strong doctrine of divine providence becomes impossible. But such a viewpoint can make no sense whatsoever of scriptural passages such as those cited above. Consider the account of Saul's death in 1 Samuel 31:1-6 and 1 Chronicles 10:8-12. Both writers describe Saul's death at his own hand in lieu of surrender to the Philistines. But then the Chronicler adds the stunning comment: "Therefore the Lord put him to death and turned the kingdom over to David the son of Jesse" (1 Chron. 10:14b). Now how is the Openness theologian to make sense of this assertion? Saul's suicide was considered a sinful and disgraceful deed and therefore could not have been causally determined by God. *Yet his suicide, says the Chronicler, was God's doing.* Or think of Joseph's statement to his brothers in Egypt: "Do not be grieved or angry with yourselves because you sold me here; for God sent me before you to preserve life . . . . You meant evil against me, but God meant it for good in order to bring about this present result" (Gen. 45:5; 50:20). Again, the brothers' treachery and deceit could not have been caused by God; and yet God sovereignly directed events toward His previsioned end of saving Israel from famine. Openness theology is at a loss to explain this coalescence of human freedom and divine sovereignty. Ironically, openness theology is forced to revert to theological determinism to account for God's providence and thus actually winds up destroying human freedom. By contrast, Molinism provides a clear account of divine sovereignty and human freedom in terms of God's middle knowledge.

Sometimes Openness theologians are fond of comparing God to a Grand Master in chess, who is able on the basis of His knowledge of His own prowess and His opponent's weakness to predict exactly when and with what move He will checkmate His opponent. The analogy is an engaging one; unfortunately, on the Openness view God is not so brilliant a chess player as to be able to know that His plans will probably succeed. For He failed to achieve the universal salvation He desired and regretted having created man. Those are not the moves of a Grand Master! So how could He possibly know before the foundations of the world, for example, that His plan for Christ to be crucified through the free agency of Pilate and Herod would be fulfilled?

By contrast, the Molinist can explain the absence of universal salvation in terms of the wrong counterfactuals' being true. It may be that a world having more saved but fewer damned than the actual world was not feasible for God. But given His knowledge of counterfactuals concerning creatures' free choices, God is certain that His plans to actualize the feasible world of His choice will be achieved. He is thus like a Grand Master who is playing an opponent whom He knows so well that He knows every move His opponent would make in response to His own moves. Such a Grand Master could not actualize just any possible match, given his opponent's freedom, but he could actualize any feasible match. The chess analogy also has relevance to the problem of suffering and evil. On the Openness view the Not-So-Grand Master will churn up a lot of unforeseen, unnecessary, and pointless suffering as he plays the game, but on the Molinist view such suffering will be permitted only in light of the Master's ultimate purpose—namely, building the Kingdom of God. Thus, we can rest assured that God has morally sufficient reasons for permitting the evils in the world, such as the World Trade Center's being destroyed, whereas on the Openness view it becomes inexplicable why God does not intervene to stop the terrorists once they have begun their crime. *The cognitively limited deity of Openness theology thus makes the problem of evil worse, not easier, for it becomes inexplicable why God just sits by wringing His hands while letting evils go on unchecked without any morally sufficient reason for not stopping them.*

The perspective of *theological determinism* interprets the passages such as those quoted above to mean that foreknowledge is based upon foreordination. God knows what will happen because He makes it happen. Knowing the intentions of His will and His almighty power, God knows that all His purpose shall be accomplished. But this interpretation inevitably makes God the author of sin, since it is He who moved Judas, for example, to betray Christ, a sin which merits everlasting perdition for the hapless Judas.

But how can a holy God move people to commit moral evil and, moreover, how can these people then be held morally responsible for acts over which they had no control? The theological determinist view seems, in effect, to move in the direction of turning God into the devil.

Even the proponent of *simple foreknowledge* (e.g., philosopher David Hunt) can make no good sense of God's providential planning of a world of free creatures in the absence of middle knowledge. For on such a view God has, logically prior to the divine decree, only natural knowledge of all the possible scenarios, but no knowledge of what would happen under any circumstances. Thus, logically posterior to the divine decree, God must consider Himself extraordinarily lucky to find that this world happened to exist. "What a break!" we can imagine God's saying to Himself, "Herod and Pilate and all those people each reacted just perfectly!" Actually, the situation is much worse than that, for God had no idea whether Herod or Pilate or the Israelite nation or the Roman Empire would even exist posterior to the divine decree. Indeed, God must be astonished to find Himself existing in a world, out of all the possible worlds He could have created, in which mankind falls into sin and God Himself enters human history as a substitutionary sacrificial offering to rescue them! Of course, one is speaking anthropomorphically here; but the point remains that without middle knowledge, God cannot know prior to the creative decree what the world would be like. If the defender of simple foreknowledge goes on to say that God's foreordination of future events is based upon His simple foreknowledge, then this trivializes the doctrine of foreordination, making it a fifth wheel which carries no load, since, as we have seen, the future by definition cannot be changed. Once God knows that an event really is future, there is nothing more left to do; foreordination becomes a redundancy. Surely, there is more substance to the biblical doctrine of foreordination than the triviality that God decrees that what will happen will happen!

Thus, of the options available, the Molinist approach provides the most elucidating account of divine providence. It enables us to embrace divine sovereignty and human freedom without mysticism or mental reservation, thereby preserving faithfully the biblical text's affirmation of both these doctrines. We therefore have powerful theological motivation for adopting the doctrine of divine middle knowledge.

### *Philosophical Argument*

Finally, we also have good philosophical grounds for thinking that a doctrine of middle knowledge is correct. For as an omniscient being, God must know all truths. Since there are counterfactual truths, God must know these. Now such truths are known by God either explanatorily prior to His decree to create the world or only posterior to His creative decree. But they cannot be known only posterior to His creative decree, since in that case it is God who decrees what choices agents shall make in whatever circumstances they find themselves, and human freedom is annihilated. Therefore, God must know counterfactuals of creaturely freedom logically prior to His creative decree, which is to say that God has middle knowledge.

We may formulate this argument as follows:

1. If there are true counterfactuals of creaturely freedom, then God knows these truths.
2. There are true counterfactuals of creaturely freedom.
3. If God knows true counterfactuals of creaturely freedom, God knows them either logically prior to the divine creative decree or only logically posterior to the divine creative decree.
4. Counterfactuals of creaturely freedom cannot be known only logically posterior to the divine creative decree.

From (1) and (2) it follows logically that

5. Therefore, God knows true counterfactuals of creaturely freedom.

From (3) and (5), it follows that

> 6. Therefore, God knows true counterfactuals of creaturely freedom either logically prior to the divine creative decree or only logically posterior to the divine creative decree.

And from (4) and (6) it follows that

> 7. Therefore, God knows true counterfactuals of creaturely freedom logically prior to the divine creative decree.

—which is the essence of the doctrine of divine middle knowledge. Let us say a word in defense of each of the argument's premises.

The truth of premise (1) is required by the standard definition of omniscience:

> O. P is omniscient = If $p$ is true, then P knows that $p$ and does not believe that not-$p$.

(O) entails that if there are counterfactual truths, then an omniscient being must know them. We have already seen the failure of revisionists to craft acceptable alternatives to (O) that would exempt an omniscient being from knowing all truths. Therefore, premise (1) is securely established.

Premise (2) asserts that there are true counterfactuals of creaturely freedom. This premise does not require us to believe that all counterfactuals about creatures' free acts are either true or false. But it does seem plausible that counterfactuals of the following form are either true or false (letting $P$ be any person, $A$ some action, and $C$ any set of circumstances including the whole history of the world up until the point of decision):

> CCF. If $P$ were in $C$, $P$ would freely do $A$.

It is counterfactuals of this form that we dignify with the title "counterfactuals of creaturely freedom" (CCF).

We have every reason to think that there are true counterfactuals of creaturely freedom. In the first place, it is *plausible that counterfactuals of the form (CCF) are true or false*. For since the circumstances mentioned in the antecedent ("if . . .") in which *P* finds himself are fully specified, any ambiguity that might cause us to doubt that the counterfactual has a truth value is removed. And it is plausible that in many cases *P* would freely do *A* in *C*, just as the counterfactual states. Second, *we ourselves often know the truth of counterfactuals about how people would act or react under particular circumstances*. While we may not know such truths with certainty, we constantly make decisions and act on the basis of which counterfactuals we think are probably true. A little reflection reveals how pervasive and indispensable such counterfactual truths are to rational conduct and planning. We sometimes base our very lives upon their truth or falsity. Third, as pointed out above, *Scripture itself gives examples of such true counterfactuals* (think again about Paul's statement in 1 Cor. 2:8: "for if they had [understood], they would not have crucified the Lord of glory"). The most common objection urged against the truth of counterfactuals of creaturely freedom is the so-called *"grounding objection."* The basic complaint here is that there is nothing to make such counterfactuals true (since they are supposed to be true logically prior to God's creative decree and even now are usually contrary-to-fact); but without a ground of their truth, they cannot be true.

Thomas Flint, an eminent defender of middle knowledge, has rightly observed that the grounding objection is, in the minds of many philosophers, the principal obstacle to endorsing a Molinist perspective.[21] It is therefore all the more remarkable that *this objection is virtually never articulated or defended in any depth by its advocates*. No detractor of the doctrine has yet responded to Alvin Plantinga's simple retort: "It seems to me much clearer that some counterfactuals of freedom are at least possibly true than that the truth of propositions must, in general, be grounded in this way."[22] What Plantinga understands—and the grounding objectors generally do not—is that behind the grounding objection sticks a theory about the relationship of truth and reality which is both subtle and controversial and which needs to be articulated, defended, and applied to counterfactuals of creaturely freedom if the grounding objection is to have any force. The detractors of middle knowledge have not even begun to address these issues.

The theory presupposed by the grounding objection is a particular construal of truth as correspondence known among contemporary philosophers as the theory of *truth-makers*.[23]   According to a view of truth as correspondence, a statement is true if and only if reality is as that statement describes. In order to identify the reality corresponding to a true statement, one typically employs a method called disquotation:  the statement "Snow is white," for example, is true if and only if snow is white. During the revival of the correspondence theory of truth in the early part of the twentieth century, philosophers such as Bertrand Russell and Ludwig Wittgenstein maintained that there must exist not only truth-bearers (whether these be sentences or thoughts or propositions or what have you) that have the property of being true and so of corresponding with reality; there must also be something in reality in virtue of which the sentences or propositions are true. This interpretation of the correspondence theory was taken up again in the 1980s as the theory of truth-makers.

A truth-maker may be defined as *that in virtue of which a sentence and/or proposition is true.* Immediately we see the potentially misleading connotations of the term "truth-maker." For *making* sounds like a causal relation involving some concrete object, but truth-makers are not normally so conceived by their advocates. Instead truth-makers are typically construed to be abstract realities like "facts" or "states of affairs"—more often than not, the fact stated as the truth conditions of a proposition. Thus, what makes the statement "Snow is white" true is the fact that snow is white or the state of affairs of snow's being white. Such abstract entities do not stand in causal relations. This invalidates at a single swoop the crude construal of the grounding objection such as comes to expression in Robert Adams' demand, "Who or what does cause them [counterfactuals of creaturely freedom] to be true?"[24]   The question is inept because *the relation between a proposition and its truth-maker is not a causal relation.*

The grounding objector seems to think that in order to be true counterfactuals of creaturely freedom must have truth-makers that either are or imply the existence of physical objects. But this assumption seems quite unwarranted, since we can think of other types of possibly true statements whose truth-makers neither are nor imply physical objects, for example:

1. No physical objects exist.
2. Dinosaurs are extinct today.
3. All ravens are black.
4. Torturing a child is wrong.
5. Napoleon lost the Battle of Waterloo.
6. The President in 2070 will be a woman.
7. If a rigid rod were placed in uniform motion through the aether, it would suffer a Lorentz-FitzGerald contraction.

Statement (1) could be true and statement (2) is true, yet they preclude the existence of truth-makers which imply the relevant physical objects, such as dinosaurs. Statement (3) is a universal statement that does not apply just to any ravens which happen to exist now and so cannot be made true just by any existing ravens' being black. Statement (4) is a value-judgment that implies neither that children do exist nor that any are actually tortured. Statements (5) and (6) are true tensed statements about persons who no longer or do not yet exist and so cannot have such persons among their truth-makers. Finally, statement (7) is a true counterfactual about the aether of nineteenth century physics, which does not exist. These statements reveal just how naïve an understanding grounding objectors have of the notion of truth-makers. For if these statements have truth-makers, their truth-makers are not physical objects out there in the world, but abstract entities like states of affairs or facts.

It is a matter of debate whether true statements do have truth-makers. In a recent critique, Greg Restall demonstrates that given the customary axioms of truth-maker theory, it follows that every true proposition is made true by every truth-maker there is, so that, for example, *Grass is green* is made true by snow's being white. In the understatement of the year, Restall muses, "This is clearly not acceptable for any philosophically discriminating account of truth makers."[25] (Restall offers an account of truth-makers involving abstract entities to solve this problem but in doing so leaves his truth-makers undefined. This result only underscores how clumsy a handling of truth-makers is presupposed by grounding objectors to middle knowledge.) Truth-maker theorists typically deny the doctrine of *truth-maker maximalism*, the doctrine that every true statement has a truth-maker. *No argument has ever been offered for the conclusion that counterfactuals of creaturely freedom cannot be among those types of truths lacking a truth-maker.* In deed, when one reflects on the fact that they are *counterfactual*, then such statements seem prime candidates for that type of statement that is true without any truth-maker.

If there are, on the other hand, truth-makers for counterfactuals of creaturely freedom, then the most obvious and plausible candidates are the facts or states of affairs disclosed by the disquotation principle. Thus, what makes it true that "If Jones were rich, he would buy a Mercedes" is the fact that if Jones were rich, he would buy a Mercedes. *Just as there are tensed facts that now exist, even though the objects and events they are about do not* (as illustrated by statements [5] and [6] above), so *there are counterfacts that actually exist, even though the objects and events they are about do not.* If counterfactuals of creaturely freedom have truth-makers, then it is in virtue of these facts or states of affairs that the corresponding statements are true. And since these counterfacts are not the result of God's decree, they exist even logically prior to God's decree to create any physical objects.

In short, Plantinga seems quite justified in being far more confident that there are true counterfactuals of creaturely freedom than that a theory which requires that they have truth-makers is true. And even if they do have truth-makers, no reason has been given why these cannot be the facts or states of affairs that are stated as their truth conditions.

Premise (3) of the argument for middle knowledge states logically exhaustive alternatives for an omniscient deity and so must be true: counterfactuals of creaturely freedom are known by God either prior to His decree or only after His decree.

Finally, premise (4) must be true because if counterfactuals of creaturely freedom were known only after the divine decree, then it is God who determined what every creature would do in every circumstance. Theological determinists bear witness to the truth of this premise in their claim that all our acts, though voluntary, are causally determined. They thereby testify that God's all-determining decree precludes libertarian freedom, which is the sort of freedom with which we are here concerned. Thus, if God knows counterfactual truths about us only posterior to His decree, then there really are no counterfactuals of creaturely freedom. If there are such counterfactuals, they must be true logically prior to the divine decree.

Given the truth of the premises, the conclusion follows that prior to His creative decree God knows all true counterfactuals of creaturely freedom, which is to say that He has middle knowledge.

Via His middle knowledge, then, God can have complete knowledge of both conditional future contingents and absolute future contingents. Such knowledge gives Him sweeping sovereignty over the affairs of men. And yet, such an account of God's knowledge is wholly compatible with human freedom, since the circumstances envisioned in counterfactuals of creaturely freedom are non-determining, and, hence, freedom-preserving. It is because of these powerful theological advantages that a Molinist account of divine omniscience constitutes the most potent antidote to the doctrine of God set forth by Openness theology.

# CONCLUSION

In conclusion, we have seen that an assessment of the biblical data leads to the conclusion that God's knowledge encompasses knowledge of both future contingents and conditional future contingents. Attempts to avoid this conclusion are rooted in a naïve hermeneutical approach to Scripture and cannot plausibly account for the many passages which either teach or illustrate God's foreknowledge and hypothetical knowledge.

From a philosophical point of view, God, as the greatest conceivable being, must be omniscient and must therefore know all truths. If, then, there are true future-tense propositions and counterfactuals of creaturely freedom, God must know them. Attempts to deny that future-tense propositions are true (or false) face serious objections; there are, on the contrary, good grounds for thinking that there are true future-tense propositions as well as true counterfactuals of creaturely freedom. Although revisionists have sometimes maintained that God can still be omniscient despite ignorance of future-tense and counterfactual truths, their re-definitions of omniscience are inadequate and in the end fail to solve the problem because God turns out not to be omniscient even on their revised definitions.

Fatalistic arguments against divine foreknowledge are either invalid or unsound, and demands for a basis of God's knowledge of future contingent truths are illicitly predicated upon a perceptualist model of divine cognition which we have no reason to accept.

Divine middle knowledge is theologically necessary for a robust, biblically faithful account of divine providence. Objections to divine middle knowledge on the basis of there being no ground of the truth of counterfactuals of creaturely freedom are rooted in an implicit and controversial theory about truth-makers which one is under no obligation to accept. Moreover, not only is it unclear why counterfactuals of freedom must have truth-makers, but plausible truth-makers for such statements can be offered.

In short, there are no adequate grounds for rejecting the testimony of both Scripture and reason to the truth of the doctrine of divine omniscience and, in particular, God's knowledge of future free acts of men.

# ENDNOTES

[1] Scripture references are in the Revised Standard Version (RSV) or the English Standard Version (ESV).

[2] Stephen Charnock, *The Existence and Attributes of God*, vol. 1 (1682; reprint, Grand Rapids: Baker, 1979), 431-32.

[3] Ben Witherington calls these conditional prophecies: *Jesus the Seer* (Peabody, Mass.: Hendrickson, 1999), 3.

[4] For the following definition see William Hasker, "A Philosophical Perspective," in Clark Pinnock, Richard Rice, John Sanders, William Hasker, and David Basinger, *The Openness of God: A Biblical Challenge to the Traditional Understanding of God* (Downer's Grove, Ill: InterVarsity Press, 1994), 136.

[5] For those unfamiliar with such terminology, a possible world does not mean another planet or universe. Rather a possible world is a way reality as a whole might be. We can think of a possible world as a huge conjunction of all propositions that could be true together. Thus, we can imagine a possible world in which the proposition "Ravi Zacharias is a poor Indian peasant" is true. That is a different possible world than the world which is actual.

[6] Modal terms have to do with what is possible rather than simply actual. For example, *being flammable* is a modal notion that does not imply that something is actually on fire.

[7] If all this were not enough, the revisionist's position is ultimately logically incoherent. For he agrees that it is logically possible to know any true, present-tense proposition. But if future-tense propositions are true or false, then there are present-tense propositions like "The future-tense proposition $p$ is presently true" which must be known to God. It cannot reasonably be denied that God must know such present-tense propositions. For God knows what properties presently inhere in existing things. But then He must know that "Truth presently inheres in

future-tense proposition *p*." Hence, the detractor of divine foreknowledge cannot coherently affirm that there are true future-tense propositions and yet deny that God knows such propositions—rather, he must deny the truth or falsity of future-tense propositions. That is to say, he must deny premise (4) of out argument.

[8] Nicholas Rescher, *Many-Valued Logic* (New York: McGraw-Hill, 1969), 2-3.

[9] Susan Haack, "On a Theological Argument for Fatalism," *Philosophical Quarterly* 24 (1974): 158.

[10] See Harry Frankfurt, "Alternative Possibilities and Moral Responsibility," *Journal of Philosophy* 66 (1969): 829-39; Thomas V. Morris, *The Logic of God Incarnate* (Ithaca, N.Y.: Cornell University Press, 1986), 151-2. For an application to theological fatalism see David P. Hunt, "On Augustine's Way Out," *Faith and Philosophy* 16 (1999): 3-26.

[11] See, for example, Alfred J. Freddoso, "Accidental Necessity and Logical Determinism," *Journal of Philosophy* 80 (1983): 257-78.

[12] See discussion in my *The Only Wise God* (Grand Rapids, Mich.: Baker, 1987; rep. ed.: Eugene, Ore.: Wipf & Stock, 2000).

[13] See my companion volumes *The Tensed Theory of Time: A Critical Examination* and *The Tenseless Theory of Time: A Critical Examination*, both with Kluwer Academic Publishers. For a popularization, see my *Time and Eternity* (Wheaton, Ill.: Crossway, 2001).

[14] Notice, however, that if we think of propositions as being within God's purview, then even on a perceptualist model, God can know the future. For He perceives which future-tense propositions presently have the property of truth inhering in them. Thus, by means of His perception of presently existing realities, He knows the truth about the future.

[15] William Lane Craig, "'No Other Name': A Middle Knowledge Perspective on the Exclusivity of Salvation through Christ," *Faith and Philosophy* 6 (1989): 172-88.

[16] William Lane Craig, "'Lest Anyone Should Fall': A Middle Knowledge Perspective on Perseverance

and Apostolic Warnings," *International Journal for Philosophy of Religion* 29 (1991): 65-74.

[17] William Lane Craig, "'Men Moved by the Holy Spirit Spoke from God' (2 Peter 1:2): A Middle Knowledge Perspective on Biblical Inspiration," *Philosophia Christi* 1 (1999): 45-82.

[18] Thomas Flint, "Middle Knowledge and the Doctrine of Infallibility," *Philosophical Perspectives*, vol. 5: *Philosophy of Religion*, ed. Jas. E. Tomberlin (Atascadero, Calif.: Ridgeway Publishing, 1991), 373-93.

[19] Thomas P. Flint, "'A Death He Freely Accepted': Molinist Reflections on the Incarnation," *Faith and Philosophy* 18 (2001): 3-20.

[20] Del Ratzsch, "Design, Chance, and Theistic Evolution," in *Mere Creation*, ed. William Dembski (Downer's Grove, Ill.: Inter Varsity, 1998), 289-312.

[21] Thomas P. Flint, *Divine Providence*, Cornell Studies in the Philosophy of Religion (Ithaca, N.Y.: Cornell University Press, 1998), 123.

[22] Alvin Plantinga, "Reply to Robert Adams," in *Alvin Plantinga*, ed. Jas. E. Tomberlin and Peter van Inwagen, Profiles 5 (Dordrecht: D. Reidel, 1985), 378.

[23] See the seminal article by Kevin Mulligan, Peter Simons, and Barry Smith, "Truth-Makers," *Philosophy and Phenomenological Research* 44 (1984): 287-321.

[24] Robert Adams, "Plantinga on the Problem of Evil," in *Alvin Plantinga*, 232. Cf. William Hasker's demand: "Who or what is it (if anything) that brings it about that these propositions are true?" (William Hasker, "A Refutation of Middle Knowledge," *Nous* 20 [1986]: 547).

[25] Greg Restall, "Truthmakers, Entailment and Necessity," *Australasian Journal of Philosophy* 74 (1996): 334.

# SUGGESTED FURTHER READING

Beilby, James K. and Paul R. Eddy, eds. *Divine Foreknowledge: Four Views.* Downers Grove, Ill.: InterVarsity Press, 2001. This book offers a presentation of and an interchange on four different views on the nature of divine foreknowledge, including open theism, simple foreknowledge, middle knowledge, and foreordination. (Popular level)

Craig, William Lane. *The Only Wise God: The Compatibility of Divine Foreknowledge and Human Freedom.* Eugene, Ore.: Wipf and Stock, 2000. A defense the idea that God is perfectly all-knowing and that divine foreknowledge and human freedom are compatible. (Popular level/Intermediate)

Fischer, John Martin, ed. God, *Foreknowledge, and Freedom.* Stanford: Stanford University Press, 1992. A reader offering wide-ranging but important articles on the question of God's foreknowledge and human freedom. (Advanced)

Hasker, William, David Basinger, and Eef Decker, eds. *Middle Knowledge: Theory and Applications* (New York: Peter Lang, 2000). A fine collection of articles on divine middle knowledge and its theological implications. (Advanced)

Flint, Thomas P. *Divine Providence: The Molinist Account.* Ithaca, N.Y.: Cornell University Press, 1998. A thorough examination of the doctrine of divine providence from a middle-knowledge perspective. (Advanced)

Kvanvig, Jonathan. *The Possibility of an All Knowing God.* New York: Macmillan, 1986. An excellent defense of God's knowledge of future contingents. (Advanced)